TRIALS OF THE STATE

Law and the Decline of Politics

Jonathan Sumption

P

PROFILE BOOKS

This paperback edition published in 2020

First published in Great Britain in 2019 by
PROFILE BOOKS LTD
29 Cloth Fair
London ECIA 7JQ
www.profilebooks.com

This book is based on the BBC Reith Lectures 2019,
first broadcast on BBC Radio 4

Copyright © Jonathan Sumption, 2019, 2020

1 3 5 7 9 10 8 6 4 2

Typeset in Dante by MacGuru Ltd
Printed and bound in Great Britain by CPI
Group (UK) Ltd, Croydon CRO 4YY

A CIP catalogue record for this book is
available from the British Library.

ISBN 978 1 78816 373 6
eISBN 978 1 78283 622 3

To the next generation

Contents

Preface

This book is based on the five BBC Reith Lectures broadcast on Radio 4 in May and June 2019. It substantially reproduces the text of the lectures, with additions and modifications provoked by the discussions which followed, and some expansion of points that could not be accommodated within the half-hour broadcasting slots.

The subtitle, *Law and the Decline of Politics*, fairly describes the contents. The law is the tool by which the state imposes its will. A lawyer's job is to say what the law is. But I am interested in a different and more fundamental question, which lawyers rarely ask themselves. Once we have found out what the law is, what makes it legitimate? Democratic institutions once lent legitimacy to laws, even in the eyes of those who disagreed with them. But for a number of years, public confidence in them has been draining away. The alternatives are some form of autocracy and a regime of judge-made law. *Trials of the State* presents thoughts which have developed in my mind over a number of years, but which the BBC series prompted me to present in a rather more disciplined form.

We are all prisoners of our own experience. I have passed most of my life in the study and teaching of history and in the work of the English courts. Lawyers live on the margins of politics, whether they like it or not. My own lifetime has witnessed radical changes in Britain's internal life and its place in the world, which have had a transformative impact on British politics. These are not claims to universal expertise. But they are not a bad starting-point. After all, none of the questions that I have posed is new. The competing claims of law, ideology and politics to legitimacy have been explored by academic lawyers and political scientists for many years. Britain's collective experience of these issues goes back a long way. Our institutions and our legal and parliamentary cultures have the longest continuous history in the world. Yet recent events have tested them. The debates on Britain's relations with the European Union have brought to a head many constitutional issues that were latent for years before the referendum of 2016.

I am grateful to Gwyneth Williams, until recently Controller of BBC Radio 4, who invited me to deliver the 2019 Reith Lectures, and to the dedicated and professional team at the BBC, in particular presenter Anita Anand, producer Jim Frank and editor Hugh Levinson. Friends and colleagues with whom I have discussed these questions have contributed more than they can ever realise to the result, although they will not necessarily agree with my views. Some of them were kind enough to criticise early drafts of the lectures, an essential process from which I have gained a great deal. My biggest debt, however, is as always to my wife, Teresa, who has lived with these lectures for almost as long as I have, and saved me from countless obscurities and solecisms.

Jonathan Sumption
June 2019

I

LAW'S EXPANDING EMPIRE

In the beginning, there was chaos and brute force, a world without law. In the mythology of ancient Athens, Agamemnon sacrificed his daughter so that the gods would allow his fleet to sail against Troy. His wife murdered him to avenge the deed, and she in turn was murdered by her son. Athena, the goddess of wisdom, put an end to the cycle of violence by creating a court to impose a solution, in what today we would call the public interest: a solution based on reason, on the experience of human frailty and on fear of the alternative. In the final part of Aeschylus' great trilogy the *Oresteia*, the goddess justifies her intervention in the world of mortals in these words: 'Let no man live uncurbed by law, nor curbed by tyranny.' That was written in the fifth century BC. But the message is timeless and universal. Law is not just an instrument of corrective or distributive justice. It is an expression of collective values and an alternative to capricious violence and despotism.

It is a vice of lawyers that they think and talk about law as if it was a self-contained subject, something to be examined like a laboratory specimen in a test-tube. But law does not occupy a world of its own.

It is part of a larger system of public decision-making. The rest is politics: the politics of ministers and legislators, of political parties, of media and pressure groups and of the wider electorate. My subject is the place of law in public life. The twin themes which I want to explore are the decline of politics and the rise of law to fill the void. What ought to be the role of law in a representative democracy like ours? Is there too much law? Is there, perhaps, too little? Do judges have too much power? What do we mean by the rule of law, the phrase which so readily trips off the tongues of lawyers? Is it, as cynics have suggested, really no more than a euphemism for the rule of lawyers?

The expanding empire of law is one of the most significant phenomena of our time. Until the nineteenth century, most human social interactions were governed by custom and convention. The law dealt with a very narrow range of human problems. It regulated title to property. It enforced contracts. It protected people's lives, their persons, their liberty and their property against arbitrary injury. But that was about all. Today, law penetrates every corner of human life. The standard modern edition of the English statutes fills 50 stout volumes, with more than 30 volumes of supplements. In addition, there are currently about 21,000 regulations made by ministers under statutory powers and nearly 12,000 regulations made by the European Union. In a single year, ending in May 2010, more than 700 new criminal offences were created, three-quarters of them by government regulation. That was admittedly a bumper year, but the rate of increase continues to be high.

On top of that, there is the relentless output of judgements of the courts, many of them on subjects that were hardly touched by law a century ago. The powers of the family courts now extend to every aspect of the well-being of children, which once belonged to the enclosed domain of the home. Complex codes of law, enforced by specialised tribunals, regulate the world of employment. An elaborate system of administrative law, largely developed by judges since the 1960s, governs most aspects of the relations between government and the citizen. The special areas which were once thought to be outside the purview of the courts, such as foreign policy, the conduct of overseas military operations and the other prerogative powers of the state, have one by one yielded to the power of judges. Above all, since 2000 a code of legally enforceable human rights has opened up vast new areas to judicial regulation. The impact of these changes can be measured by the growth of the legal profession. In 1911 there was one solicitor in England for every 3,000 inhabitants. Just over a century later, there is about one for every 400, a sevenfold increase.

The rule of law is one of those clichés of modern life which tends to be invoked, even by lawyers, without much reflection on what it actually means. The essence of it can be summed up in three points. First, public authorities have no power to coerce us, other than what the law gives them. Second, people must have a minimum of basic legal rights. One can argue about what those rights should be. But they must at least include protection from physical violence and from arbitrary interference with life, liberty and property. Without these, social existence is no more than an exercise of raw power. Third, there must be access to independent judges to vindicate these rights, administer the criminal law and enforce the limits of state power. At least as important as these, however, is a clear understanding of what the rule of law does not mean. It does not mean that every human problem and every moral dilemma calls for a legal solution. So why has this vast expansion of the domain of law happened?

The fundamental reason is the arrival of a broadly based democracy between the 1860s and the 1920s. Mass involvement in public affairs has inevitably led to rising demands on the state: as the provider of amenities, as a guarantor of minimum standards of security and as a regulator of economic activity. Optimism about what collective action can achieve is natural to social animals. In Britain, this feeling was intensified by the experience of two world wars in which the state mobilised resources on an unprecedented scale towards a single objective. The impressive results enhanced its prestige and suggested that the same effort might successfully be applied to the arts of peace. Confidence in the benign power of collective action to improve the lot of humanity was the biggest single factor in the landslide election of a Labour government in 1945. Law is the prime instrument of collective action. Rising expectations of what it can achieve lead naturally to calls for legal solutions.

In some areas, this is dictated by the very nature of the problem. Consider, for example, the unwelcome side-effects of technological and economic change, which economists call 'externalities': industrial sickness and injury, pollution, monopoly and climate change, to name only some of the more obvious ones. Economic growth is the spontaneous creation of numberless individuals. But spontaneous action cannot address the unwanted collective costs that go with it. Only the state can do that. So we have laws against cartels, pollution and so on. However, there are other areas where the intervention of law is not forced on us. It is a collective choice, which reflects pervasive changes in our outlook. I want to draw attention to two of these changes, which have contributed a great deal to the expansion of law's empire. One is a growing moral and social absolutism which looks to law to produce social and moral conformity. The other is the continual quest for greater security and reduced risk.

Let us look first at law as a means of imposing conformity. This was once regarded as one of its prime functions. The law regulated religious worship until the eighteenth century. It discriminated between different religious denominations until the nineteenth. It regulated private and consensual sexual relations until quite recently. Homosexual acts were criminal until 1967. Today the law has almost entirely withdrawn from these areas. Indeed, it has moved to the opposite extreme and banned the discrimination that was once compulsory. Yet in other respects we have moved back to the older idea that law exists to impose conformity. We live in a censorious age – more so, perhaps, than at any time since the evangelical movement transformed the moral sensibilities of the Victorians. Liberal voices in Victorian Britain, such as John Stuart Mill, were the first to protest against the implications for personal liberty. Law, he argued, exists to protect us from harm, not to recruit us to moral conformity. Yet today a hectoring press can discharge an avalanche of public scorn and abuse on anyone who steps out of line. Social media encourage a resort to easy answers, and generate a powerful herd instinct which suppresses not just dissent but doubt and nuance as well. Public and even private solecisms can destroy a person's livelihood. Advertisers pressurise editors not to publish controversial pieces, and editors are sacked for persisting. Student organisations can prevent unorthodox speakers from being heard. It has even been suggested that the mere presentation of opinions to young people which are fundamentally opposed to their own is a threat to their emotional security from which they are entitled to be protected. These things have made the pressure to conform more intense than it ever was in Mill's day. It is the same mentality which looks to law to regulate areas of life that once belonged exclusively to the domain of personal judgement. We are a lot less ready than we were to respect the autonomy of an individual's choices. We tend to regard social and moral values as belonging to the community as a whole, as matters for collective and not personal decision.

In 2017, the courts and the press were much exercised by the case of Charlie Gard, a baby who had been born with a rare and fatal genetic disease. The medical advice was that there was no appreciable chance of improvement. The hospital where he was being treated applied to the High Court for permission to withdraw treatment and allow him to die. The child's parents rejected the medical advice. They wanted to take him out of the hands of the NHS and move him to the United States so that he could receive an untested experimental treatment there. The American specialist thought that the chances of improvement were small, but better than zero. The parents wanted to take the chance. Unusually, they had raised the money by crowdfunding, and were able to pay the cost without resorting to public funds. The case raised a difficult combination of moral judgement and pragmatic welfare. The courts authorised the hospital to withdraw therapeutic treatment, and the child died.*

There are two striking features of this story. The first is that, although the decision whether to continue treatment was a matter of clinical judgement, the clinicians involved were unwilling to make that judgement on their own, as I suspect they would have done a generation before. They wanted the endorsement of a judge. This was not because judges were thought to have any special clinical or moral qualifications that the doctors lacked. It was because judges have a power of absolution. By passing the matter to the courts the doctors sheltered themselves from legal liability. That is an understandable instinct. Doctors do not want to run the risk of being sued or prosecuted, however confident they are of their

---

* *Great Ormond Street Hospital for Children NHS Foundation Trust v. Yates* [2017] 4 WLUK 260; [2018] 4 WLR 5.

judgement. But the risk of being sued or prosecuted only exists because we have come to regard these terrible human dilemmas as the proper domain of law. The second feature of the case is perhaps even more striking. The courts ruled that not only should the hospital be entitled to withdraw therapeutic treatment, but that the parents should not be permitted to take the chance of a cure elsewhere. It was not suggested that moving him to the United States and treating him there would actually worsen his awful situation, although it would obviously have prolonged it. The parents' judgement seems to have been within the broad range of judgements that responsible and caring parents could make. Yet in law it was ultimately a matter for an organ of the state, namely the Family Division of the High Court. The parents' decision was, so to speak, nationalised. I am certainly not criticising this decision. I only point out that the answer would probably have been different a generation before, if indeed the question had reached the courts at all.

I cite this agonising case because, although its facts are unusual, it is illustrative of a more general tendency of law. Rules of law and the discretionary powers which the law confers on judges limit the scope for autonomous decision-making by individuals. They cut down the area within which citizens take personal responsibility for their own destinies and those of their families. Of course, the law has always done this in some areas. The classic liberal position (again, it was John Stuart Mill who expressed it best) is that we have to distinguish between those acts which affect other people, and are therefore proper matters for legal regulation, and those which affect only the actor, which belong in his personal space. So, we criminalise murder, rape, theft and fraud. We say that the morality of these acts is not something that should be left to the conscience of every individual. Not only are they harmful to others, but there is an almost complete consensus that they are morally wrong. What is new is the growing tendency for law to regulate human choices even in cases where they do no harm to others and there is no consensus about their morality.

A good example is provided by some recent animal welfare legislation. England and Scotland, in common with some other European countries have, over the last few years, enacted laws banning fur farming. The reason is not that the farming and humane slaughter of furry animals for human use are in themselves objectionable. Most people accept that rearing and killing animals for food, for example, is morally acceptable. But we don't eat beavers or minks. The sole reason for farming them is their fur. The idea behind the statutory ban is that the desire to wear a beaver hat or a mink coat is not a morally sufficient reason for killing animals, whereas a desire to eat them would be. Yet many people would disagree with that judgement. Some of them are happy to wear fur even if others disagree. But Parliament has decreed that fur farming is not a matter on which they should be allowed to make their own moral judgements. Similar points could be made about the elaborate legislation that now regulates the docking of dogs' tails. It allows the practice where it has a utilitarian value (for working dogs, for example) but not where its only value is aesthetic (for household pets or dog shows). The underlying notion is that, although docking a dog's tail is not necessarily bad, aesthetic pleasure is not a morally sufficient reason for doing it.

I have no desire to get into an argument about the rights or wrongs of laws like these. The point that I am making is a different one. These laws are addressed to moral issues on which people hold a variety of different views. But the law regulates their moral choices on the principle that there ought to be only one collective moral judgement, not a multiplicity of individual ones. This tells us something about the changing attitude of our society to law. It marks the expansion of the public space at the expense of the private space that was once thought sacrosanct. Even when there are no compelling welfare considerations involved, we resort to law to impose uniform solutions in areas where we once tolerated a diversity of judgement and behaviour. We are afraid to let people be guided by their own moral judgements, in case they arrive at answers that we do not agree with.

Let us turn now to the other major factor behind the growing public appetite for legal rules: namely, the quest for greater security and reduced risk. This is particularly important in the areas of public order, health and safety, employment, and consumer protection, which present the main risks to our well-being and account for a high proportion of modern lawmaking.

People sometimes speak as if the elimination of risk to life, health and well-being was an absolute value. But we do not really act on that principle, either in our own lives or in our collective arrangements. Road accidents, for example, are by far the largest cause of accidental physical injury in this country. We could almost completely eliminate them by reviving the Locomotive Act of 1865, which limited the speed of motorised vehicles to 4 m.p.h. in the country and 2 m.p.h. in towns. Today we allow faster speeds, although we know for certain that it will mean that many more people are killed or injured on the roads. We do this because total safety would be too inconvenient. Difficult as it is to say so, hundreds of deaths on the roads and thousands of crippling injuries are thought to be a price worth paying for the ability to get around quicker and more comfortably. So eliminating risk is not an absolute value. It is a question of degree.

Some years ago, the courts had to deal with the case of a young man who had broken his neck by diving head-first into a shallow lake at a well-known beauty spot. He was paralysed for life. He sued the local authority for negligence. The local authority had put up warning notices. But his case was that, since they knew that people were apt to ignore the notices, they should have taken steps to close off the lake area altogether. The Court of Appeal agreed with him. But when the case reached the House of Lords, the judges pointed out that there was a price to be paid for protecting this young man from his own folly. The price was the loss of liberty which would be suffered by the great majority of people who enjoyed visiting the lake and were sensible enough to do it safely. So the claim ultimately failed.* The Law Lords had put their fingers on a wider dilemma. Every time that a public authority is blamed for failing to prevent some tragedy like this, it will tend to respond by restricting the liberty of the public at large in order to deprive them of the opportunity to harm themselves. It is the only sure way to

---

* *Tomlinson v. Congleton Borough Council* [2004] 1 AC 46.

deflect criticism. Every time that we criticise social workers for failing to stop some terrible instance of child abuse, we are in effect inviting them to intervene more readily in the lives of innocent parents in case their children too may be at risk. The law can enhance personal security. But its protection comes at a price, and it can be a heavy one. Thus we arrive at one of the supreme ironies of modern life: we have expanded the range of individual rights while at the same time drastically curtailing the scope for individual choice.

Dilemmas of this sort have existed for centuries. What has changed in recent years is the degree of risk that people are prepared to tolerate in their lives. Unlike our forebears, we are no longer willing to accept the wheel of fortune as an ordinary incident of human existence. We regard physical, financial and emotional security not just as a normal state of affairs but as an entitlement. Some people will welcome this change. Others will deplore it. Most of us probably take different views about it at different moments of our lives. But none of us should be surprised. It is a rational response to important changes in our world. Improvements in the technical competence of humanity have given us more influence over our own and other people's well-being. But they have not been matched by corresponding improvements in our moral sensibilities or our solicitude for our neighbours. Misfortunes that seemed unavoidable to our ancestors seem eminently avoidable to us. Once they are seen to be avoidable consequences of human agency, they tend to become a proper subject for the attribution of legal responsibility. So, after every disaster, we are apt to think that the law must either have been broken or be insufficiently robust. We look for a legal remedy: a lawsuit, a criminal prosecution or more legislation. 'There ought to be a law against it', is the universal cry. Usually there is, or soon will be.

Of course, the law does not in fact provide a solution for every misfortune. It expects people, within limits, to look after their own interests. It assumes that some risks may have to be accepted because the social and economic cost of eliminating them is just too high. However, public expectations are a powerful motor of legal development. Judges do not decide cases in accordance with the state of public opinion. But it is their duty to take account of the values of the society which they serve. Risk-aversion has become one of the most powerful of those values.

My purpose in making these points is not to deplore the growing impact of law in our lives. Like most people, I regard some interventions of law as desirable and others as pointless or foolish. It would be absurd to try to put the clock back to an earlier age in which life was simpler and the public had fewer expectations of the state. The advance of law is simply a fact, which it is necessary to recognise because it has important implications for the way that we govern ourselves. We cannot have more law without more state power to apply it. Today, the amount of state power available for this purpose is very great. The state has had a virtual monopoly of coercive force since the middle of the nineteenth century. Within the last thirty years the technology of surveillance and information retrieval has given it an unparalleled capacity to concentrate that force against individuals. The German sociologist Max Weber, who was the first to argue that bureaucracy was the essential feature of modern societies, also gave it a definition. 'Bureaucratic administration,' he wrote, 'means domination through knowledge.' In an age when the state can do so much more to control human behaviour, people expect this plenitude of power to be used to impose collective standards of behaviour and to enhance welfare.

The great seventeenth-century political philosopher Thomas Hobbes believed that political communities surrendered their liberty to an absolute ruler in return for security. Hobbes has few followers today. But modern societies have gone a long way towards justifying his theories. We have made a Leviathan of the state, expanding and harnessing its power in order to reduce the risks that threaten our well-being. The seventeenth century may have abolished absolute monarchy. But the twentieth century created absolute democracy in its place.

With the practical limits on state power gone, we have to rely on principle to control this great concentration of power. But what is the principle on which we should rely? What are the proper limits of state power? How are those limits to be enforced? These are not new questions. The English have debated them since the Middle Ages. But the nature of the debate is inevitably different in a democracy. Our ancestors looked upon the state as an autonomous power, embodied in a powerful monarch and his ministers. It was natural for them to talk about the relations between the state and its citizens in 'us and them' terms. But in a democracy the state is neither with us nor against us. It *is* us. This is why most of us are so ambivalent about it. We resent its power. We object to its intrusiveness. We criticise the arrogance of some of its agents and spokesmen. But our collective expectations depend for their fulfilment on its persistent intervention in almost every area of our lives. We don't like it, but we want it. The danger is that the demands of democratic majorities for state action may take forms that are profoundly objectionable, even oppressive, to individuals or whole sectors of our society.

II

IN PRAISE OF POLITICS

Politicians have had a bad press. The eighteenth-century sage Dr Samuel Johnson thought that they were only in it out of vanity and ambition. Mark Twain believed that they were corrupt as well as stupid. George Orwell famously dismissed the world of politics as a 'mass of lies, evasions, folly, hatred and schizophrenia'. Statements like these are timeless clichés, faithfully reflecting the received opinion of every age, including ours. Surviving literature and graffiti show that they were already common in the ancient world. So the title of this chapter may seem provocative. At least, I hope so. For I want to make the case for the political process, with all its imperfections. I argued in the previous chapter that the quest for protection from perceived threats to our values and well-being had immeasurably expanded the role of the state in our lives. In a democracy, the state, with its immense potential for both good and ill, is ultimately in the hands of electoral majorities. Hence comes the great dilemma of modern democracy. How do we control the potentially oppressive power of democratic majorities without undermining democracy itself?

Let us start with some basic questions. Why do people obey the state? Its coercive power, great as it is, is hardly a sufficient explanation. Fundamentally, we obey the state because we respect the legitimacy of the political order on which it is founded. Legitimacy is a vital but elusive concept in human affairs. Legitimacy is less than law but more than opinion. It is a collective instinct that we owe it to each other to accept the authority of our institutions, even when we do not like what they are doing. This depends on an unspoken sense that we are in it together. It is the result of common historical attachments, language, place and culture: in short, of collective identity. But even in an age when collective identities are under strain, legitimacy is still the basis of all consent. For all its power the modern state still depends on a large measure of tacit consent. The sudden collapse of the communist governments of eastern Europe at the end of the last century was a sobering lesson in the importance of legitimacy. Even in a totalitarian state, civil government breaks down at the point where tacit consent fails and ideology cannot fill the gap. If this was true of the party dictatorships of eastern Europe, with their intimidating apparatus of social control, how much more is it true of a relatively free society such as ours?

The legitimacy of state action in a democracy depends on a general acceptance of its decision-making processes: not necessarily of the decisions themselves, but of the method of making them. A free society comprises countless individuals and groups with conflicting opinions and interests. Some of these interests and opinions provoke strong passions. The first task of any political system is to accommodate these differences, so that people can live together in a single community without the systematic application of force. Democracies operate on the implicit basis that, although the majority has authorised policies which the minority rejects, these differences are transcended by their common acceptance of the legitimacy of its decision-making processes.

Majority rule is the basic principle of democracy. But that only means that a majority is enough to authorise the state's acts. It is not enough to make them legitimate. This is because majority rule is no more than a rule of decision. It does nothing to accommodate our differences. It just restates them in numerical terms. Democracies cannot operate on the basis that a bare majority takes 100 per cent of the political spoils. If it did, it would harbour large and permanently disaffected groups in their midst, who had no common bonds to transcend their differences with the majority. A state based on that principle would quickly cease to be a political community. This is one reason why all democracies have evolved methods of limiting or diluting the power of majorities. I am going to consider two of them. They are really the only two that matter. One is representative politics. The other is law.

Today, we could in theory abolish representation, and with it politics as we know it. For the first time since the whole citizenry of ancient Athens gathered in the *agora* to transact public business, it would be technically feasible for the electorate to vote directly on every measure. In fact, no democracy works like that. They act through elected legislatures. They do this not just for reasons of practicality, but on principle. In one of his contributions to the *Federalist Papers*, James Madison, the chief draftsman of the US constitution, gave what is still the classic justification for the representative principle. A chosen body of citizens, he thought, was less likely to sacrifice the true interests of the country to short-term considerations, unthinking impulses or sectional interests. 'Under such a regulation, it may well happen that the public voice, pronounced by the representatives of the people, will be more consonant to the public good than if pronounced by the people themselves.' In England, Madison's contemporary the politician and philosopher Edmund Burke carried this idea further. Addressing his constituents in Bristol, he said:

To deliver an opinion is the right of all men. That of Constituents is a weighty and respectable opinion, which a Representative ought always to rejoice to hear; and which he ought always most seriously to consider. But authoritative instructions, mandates issued, which the Member is bound blindly and implicitly to obey, to vote, and to argue for, though contrary to the clearest conviction of his judgement and conscience; these are things utterly unknown to the laws of this land, and which arise from a fundamental Mistake of the whole order and tenor of our Constitution. Parliament is not a Congress of Ambassadors from different and hostile interests [...] but [...] a deliberative Assembly of one Nation, with one Interest, that of the whole.

This view might be called 'elitist', and so it is. But political elites have their uses. Professional politicians can fairly be expected to bring to their work a more reflective approach, a broader outlook and a lot more information than their electors. But there is also a more fundamental point. Nations have collective interests which extend over a longer time-scale and a wider geographical range than are ever likely to be reflected in the public opinion of the moment. Today, for example, we face issues such as climate change, on which the interests of future generations differ from those of the current electorate. There are other issues on which the opinions of England, which is electorally dominant, differ from those of Scotland, Wales or Northern Ireland. Brexit is an issue that raises both of these problems. It was the eighteenth-century philosopher David Hume who first pointed to what he called the 'incurable narrowness of soul' that makes people prefer the immediate to the remote. If we are to avoid the same narrowness of soul, we have to take a view of the national interest which transcends a current snapshot of electoral opinion.

Historically, representative politics has been by far the most effective way of doing this, while at the same time accommodating the differences among our people. This is mainly because of the pivotal role of those much maligned institutions, political parties. Political parties are creatures of mass democracy. Writing at the end of the nineteenth century, when mass democracy was new, the great constitutional lawyer A. V. Dicey regarded them as conspiracies which sacrificed the public service to sectional interests. That is still a widely held view. But experience has, I think, proved it wrong. Political parties have not usually been monolithic groups. They have been coalitions of opinion, united by a loose consistency of outlook and the desire to win elections. Politics is a market-place. To achieve a critical size and command a parliamentary majority, parties have traditionally had to bid for support from a highly diverse body of MPs and an even more diverse electorate. They have had to adjust their appeal to changes in the public's sentiments or priorities that seemed likely to influence voting patterns. Their whole object is to produce a slate of policies which perhaps only a minority would have chosen as their preferred option, but which the broadest possible range of people can live with. This has traditionally made them powerful engines of national compromise and effective mediators between the state and the electorate.

In Britain, it is impossible to think about these things without an eye to the tumults that followed the referendum of 2016 on membership of the European Union. There are serious arguments for leaving the European Union and serious arguments for remaining. I am not going to express a view about either, because they are irrelevant to my theme. I want to focus on the implications for the way we govern ourselves. Brexit is an issue on which people feel strongly, and on which Britain is divided, roughly down the middle. These divisions are problematic, not just in themselves, but because they roughly correspond to other divisions in our society: generational, social, economic, educational and regional.

It is a classic case for the kind of accommodations which a representative legislature is best placed to achieve. Europe has become the defining issue which determines party allegiance for much of the electorate. As a result, we have seen both major national parties, which previously supported membership of the European Union, adjust their policy positions to the new reality. That is natural. It is what political parties have always done. In a sense, it is what they are for. But there remains a large body of opinion that is strongly opposed to Brexit. They include some of the most articulate and well-informed voices in our society. One would therefore ordinarily expect the political process to produce a compromise not entirely to the liking of either camp, but just about acceptable to both. This has proved exceptionally difficult. Why is that?

The fundamental reason is the choice of a referendum as a method of decision-making. A referendum is a device for bypassing the ordinary political process. It takes decision-making out of the hands of politicians, whose interest is generally to accommodate the widest range of opinion, and places it in the hands of individual electors, who have no reason to consider any opinion but their own. The very object of a referendum is to inhibit an independent assessment of the national interest by politicians, which is one reason why it might be thought rather absurd to criticise them for failing to do so. A referendum obstructs compromise, by producing a result in which 52 per cent of voters feel entitled to speak for the whole nation, and 48 per cent do not matter at all. This is, after all, the tacit assumption of every minister who declares that 'the British people' has approved this or that measure, as if only the majority were part of 'the British people'. It is the mentality which has created an unwarranted sense of entitlement among the sort of people who denounce those who disagree with them as 'enemies', 'traitors', 'saboteurs' or even 'Nazis'. This is the authentic language of totalitarianism. It is the lowest point to which a political community can sink short of actual violence.

Since the beginning of 2019, politics has begun to reassert itself. Parliament has moved to force compromise on those who felt that the referendum entitled them to absolute outcomes. At the time of writing, the final outcome cannot be known. But if the process has been late, slow and incomplete, it is because of another factor which has been at work for longer and may prove even more damaging. This is the steep decline in public engagement with active politics. The turn-out at general elections has been on a declining trend for many years. At one point, in 2001 it fell below 60 per cent, the lowest ever. In the early 1950s, political parties were the largest membership organisations in Britain. The Conservative Party had about 2.8 million members. The Labour Party had about 1 million members, in addition to the notional membership of those belonging to its affiliated trade unions. Between them, they probably represented a rough cross-section of the voting public. Today, in spite of the recent rise in Labour Party membership, the Royal Society for the Protection of Birds has a larger membership than all three established national parties combined. The Hansard Society's latest annual Audit of Political Engagement records a marked rise in the number of people who say that they do not want to be involved at all in either national or local decision-making. All this has widened the gap between professional politicians and the public. It has also meant that membership of political parties has been abandoned to small numbers of activists who are increasingly unrepresentative of those who vote for them. The effect has been to obstruct the ability of parties to function as instruments of compromise, and to limit the range of options on offer to the electorate. This is a dangerous position to be in. The current disengagement of so many voters is in the long run likely to lead to a far more partisan and authoritarian style of political leadership.

There are some truths that it is uncomfortable to admit, but which are nonetheless true for that.

One of them is that an important object of modern democratic constitutions is to treat the people as the source of legitimacy, while placing barriers between them and the levers of power. They do this in order to contain the fissiparous tendencies of democracy and to counter its inherent tendency to destroy itself when majorities become a source of instability and oppression. One of these barriers, as I have argued, is the concept of representation. The other is law, with its formidable bias in favour of individual rights and traditional social expectations, and a corps of professional judges to administer it who are not accountable to the electorate for their decisions. These two barriers are not mutually inconsistent. You can have both. To a greater or lesser extent, most countries do. But we need to understand the limits of what law can contribute to the task of controlling majorities, and the price to be paid if it tries too hard.

The attractions of law are obvious. Judges are generally intelligent, reflective and articulate people. They are intellectually honest. They are used to thinking seriously about problems that have no easy answer. Contrary to the familiar cliché, they know a good deal about the world. The whole judicial process is animated by a combination of abstract reasoning, social observation and ethical value-judgement that seems to many people to introduce a higher morality into public decision-making. Why not embrace it? As so often happens with our infinitely flexible, unwritten constitution, this question is being quietly answered before it has even been formally asked. As politics have lost their prestige, judges have been only too ready to fill the gap. The catch-phrase that justifies this is the 'rule of law'. But in the last half-century the courts have developed a broader concept of the rule of law, which penetrates well beyond their traditional role of deciding legal disputes and into the realms of legislative and ministerial policy.

Judges have always made law. To decide disputes between litigants, they have to fill gaps, supplying answers that cannot be found in existing legal sources. They have to be prepared to change existing judge-made rules if they are mistaken, redundant or outdated. The common law, which has grown up organically through the decisions of generations of judges, remains a major source of our law. Judges have traditionally done this within an existing framework of legal principle, and without trespassing on the functions of Parliament and the executive. In the last three decades, however, there has been a change of judicial mood. The courts have come to share the general suspicion of the political process and of political reasoning as an element in public decision-making. They have developed a broader concept of the rule of law which greatly enlarges their constitutional role. They have claimed a wider supervisory authority over other organs of the state. They have inched their way towards a notion of fundamental law overriding ordinary processes of political decision-making. If you were to sit in on an appeal in the Supreme Court on a question of public law, you would notice that in addition to the advocates of the parties there are various lawyers representing 'interveners'. These are single-issue pressure groups with highly specific political agendas. Often, they are agendas which they have failed to persuade Parliament to adopt but hope to impose through the courts. Their presence is symptomatic of a profound change in the constitutional role of the courts. To adapt the famous dictum of the German military theorist Clausewitz about war, law is now the continuation of politics by other means.

The courts operate on a principle, not always acknowledged but usually present, which lawyers call the principle of legality. It is probably better described as a principle of legitimacy. Some things are regarded as inherently illegitimate: for example, retrospective legislation, oppression of individuals, obstructing access to a court, acts contrary to international law and so on. This does not mean that Parliament cannot do them. It means that those who propose such things must squarely declare what they are doing and take the political heat. Otherwise there is too great a risk that the unacceptable implications of some loosely worded proposal will pass unnoticed as the bill goes through Parliament. The principle of legitimacy is a valuable technique for ascertaining what Parliament really intended. But it puts great power in the hands of judges. Judges decide what are the norms by which to identify particular actions as illegitimate. Judges decide what language is clear enough. These are elastic concepts. There are usually no clear legal principles to shape them. The answer depends on a subjective judgement, in which a judge's personal opinions and values are always influential and often decisive. There are those who assert that the personal opinions and values of judges are usually benign, and sometimes that may be so. But the assertion does not address the constitutional anomaly involved. If judges assert a power to give legal effect to their opinions and values, what is that but a claim to political power without political responsibility?

Let me illustrate the point with two recent decisions of the Supreme Court. Both of them concerned a matter on which the courts have always been sensitive, namely attempts to curb their own authority. As it happens, I did not sit on either of them.

The first is about court fees. Employment Tribunals were created by Act of Parliament to provide a cheap and informal way in which employees could enforce the rights conferred on them by statute. Until 2013, access to them was free. But in that year the government introduced steep fees which people on low or middling incomes could not afford – at any rate not without large sacrifices in other directions. The government had a general statutory power to charge fees. In 2017 the Supreme Court held that the language of the Act was not clear enough to authorise fees so large that many employees would be unable to enforce their rights in court.* The decision has been criticised. But I think that it was perfectly orthodox. The law must have a measure of coherence. MPs looking at the words of the bill as it went through Parliament would not have suspected that the power to charge fees under this statute would be used to stifle the rights of employees under other statutes.

I want now to move to the opposite extreme. The Freedom of Information Act entitles people to see certain categories of document held by public bodies, unless there is an overriding public interest in their being withheld. The Act conferred on a court the power to order disclosure. But it also gave ministers a veto if they considered that disclosure would be

---

R (on the application of Unison) v. Lord Chancellor [2017] 3 WLR 409.

contrary to the public interest and that the decision could be justified in Parliament. In other words, it allowed them to impose a political rather than a legal solution. The tribunal decided that letters written to ministers by the Prince of Wales should be disclosed to a journalist on *The Guardian*. Thereupon, the Attorney-General issued a certificate under the Act, overriding that decision on the ground that disclosure was not in the public interest. The Supreme Court, by a majority of 5 to 2, quashed his decision. The majority's reason, however dressed up, was that they did not approve of the power that Parliament had on the face of it conferred on ministers. Three of the judges thought that it was such a bad idea that Parliament could not really have meant what it had plainly said. Two other judges accepted that Parliament must have meant it, but thought that the Attorney-General had no right to disagree with the tribunal. For my part, I think that there is no reason why a statute should not say that on an issue like this a minister answerable to Parliament is a more appropriate judge of the public interest than a court. As one of the two dissenting judges pointed out, 'the rule of law is not the same as the rule that the courts must always prevail no matter what the statute says.'*

---

*R *(on the application of Evans) v. Attorney-General* [2015] AC 1787.

No other modern case reveals so clearly the judges' expansive view of the rule of law. Whether the Prince of Wales's letters should be disclosed is not itself a very important question. But the same technique has been applied more discreetly to sensitive issues of social policy, about which the public feels more strongly. Examples over the past half-century include education, subsidised fares on public transport, social security benefits, the use of overseas development funds, statutory defences to murder, the establishment of public enquiries and many others. On immigration and penal policy, the courts have for years applied values of their own, which are at odds with the harsher policies adopted with strong public support by Parliament and successive governments. Most people's reaction to decisions like these depends on whether they agree with the result. But we ought to care about how our decisions are made, and not just about the outcome. We ought to ask whether litigation is really the right way to resolve differences of opinion about what are really questions of policy. Next time we may not like either the procedure or the result. Many people applaud decisions of the courts that wrong-foot public authorities. Sometimes they are right to applaud. But there is a price to be paid for resolving debatable policy issues in this way.

In the first place, there is the loss of democratic

legitimacy involved. It is the proper function of the courts to stop governments exceeding or abusing their legal powers. The decision is not political, even if it has political consequences, A good example drawn from recent history is the Supreme Court's decision in January 2017 that the government did not have the power to give notice under Article 50 of the EU Treaty to withdraw from the European Union without statutory authority. The Divisional Court, which had decided the case in the same way at first instance, was widely assumed to have been guided by the judges' supposed objections to Brexit. They were memorably castigated for it in a newspaper headline ('Enemies of the People'). But although the political impact of the decision was considerable, it was an ordinary exercise of a function which the English courts had been performing since the seventeenth century. The result was an orthodox application of the long-standing constitutional rule that only Parliament can change the law.* But it is one thing for judges to keep governments within their legal powers. It is another thing altogether to allow them to circumvent Parliamentary legislation which they dislike or to review policy decisions for which minis-ters are answerable to Parliament. That is to confer

---

R (Miller) v. Secretary of State for Exiting the European Union [2018] AC 61.

vast discretionary power over truly political issues on a body of people who are not politically accountable to anyone for what they do.

In Britain, judges have been nominated by a non-political commission since 2006. But there are demands that they should be subject to political scrutiny before their appointment takes effect. The political character of much of their work may sooner or later make these demands irresistible. In the United States, the result has been the appointment of judges because of their identification with known political positions. In this country, such a change would transform the whole nature of the legal process and discredit the judges who work in it.

The judicial resolution of policy issues would also undermine the single biggest advantage of the political process, which is to accommodate the divergent interests and opinions of citizens. It is true that politics do not always perform that function well. It may be that politics are not performing it well at the moment. I have suggested some reasons for that. But judges will never be able to perform it. Litigation can rarely mediate differences. It is a zero sum game. The winners carry off the prize, and the losers pay. Litigation is not a consultative or participatory process. It is an appeal to law. Law is rational. Law is coherent. Law is analytically consistent and rigorous. But in public affairs, these are not always virtues. Opacity, inconsistency and fudge may be intellectually impure, which is why lawyers do not like them. But they are often inseparable from the kind of compromises that we have to make as a society if we are to live together in peace.

III

HUMAN RIGHTS AND WRONGS

Human rights are where law and politics meet. It can be an unfriendly meeting. A few years ago, the then Prime Minister, speaking in the House of Commons, described a recent Supreme Court judgement on human rights as 'appalling'. The same Prime Minister later said about another human rights decision that it made him 'physically sick'. 'End this human rights insanity', screamed the *Daily Mail* about the same decision. These are strong words. What is all the fuss about?

Much of the political passion surrounding human rights is generated by a small number of uncharacteristic cases on questions which generate strong feelings among the public. Notable examples include the role of human rights in obstructing the extradition of alleged criminals, preventing the deportation of illegal immigrants or moderating the impact of domestic penal policy. Some of this passion is ill informed and based on selective or misleading accounts of the facts. The Supreme Court decision that made Mr Cameron physically sick was about the statute establishing the sex offenders' register, which contained no provision for removing a name from the register in any circumstances or at any time. The court did no more than declare that a person on the register should be entitled to come off it if he could show that he no longer presented any real risk to the public.* It can fairly be said that this kind of issue is in the nature of things legislative, but the decision hardly warranted the outbreak of ministerial colic that followed. In perhaps the most controversial case of all, an alleged terrorist, Abu Qatada, managed to delay his extradition to Jordan for eleven years by successive appeals to the courts on human rights grounds. His case was that he would be tortured in Jordan, or the evidence against him would be obtained by torturing other people. But this would have been a ground for resisting extradition even before the Human Rights Act. It is hard to imagine that any civilised country would extradite someone to a place where he would be tortured or deprived of a fair trial. In fact, Abu Qatada was never prosecuted for any offence in the United Kingdom and was ultimately acquitted on all charges in Jordan.

The real problem about modern human rights law has very little to do with emotive cases like these. Human rights raise one of the most difficult and fundamental issues for any democracy. How far

---

R (F (a child) v. Secretary of State for the Home Department (Lord Advocate and another intervening) [2011] 1 AC 331.

is it legitimate for democracies to create a body of law that is independent of democratic choice and protected against abrogation or amendment by a democratic legislature? The controversy surrounding human rights in Britain is due mainly to concern that human rights law has exceeded its proper limits and begun to trespass on the proper sphere of democratic politics. I am conscious that there are some ideas that one hesitates to attack, because of the kind of allies that one is liable to attract. But this issue is too important to be ignored.

Human rights are not new. The idea is found in Roman law and in Christian theology of the Middle Ages. A quarter of a millennium ago, Sir William Blackstone, the author of the earliest methodical survey of the English common law, called them 'natural rights'. They were, he believed, recognised by the common law because they belonged to human beings by the immutable laws of nature. Blackstone's natural rights included many rights which would be regarded as human rights today, including rights to bodily integrity, property, free speech and immunity from arbitrary arrest, together with a right of access to the courts to enforce them. The idea behind this is simple and undeniably attractive. It is that there are some inalienable rights which human beings enjoy, not by the largesse of the state or the forbearance of their fellow citizens but because they are inherent in their humanity. This is the principle that underlies modern human rights theory. There are, however, some unanswered problems about it which, if we are honest, we must recognise.

To say that some rights are inherent in our humanity, without elaboration, is really no more than rhetoric. It does not get us anywhere, unless there is some way of identifying which rights are inherent in our humanity, and why. This is essentially a matter of opinion. In a democracy, differences of opinion on what rights ought to exist are resolved politically, through legislation. In recent years, English judges have rediscovered the common-law sources of human rights, and presented them as an alternative and indigenous source of protection for the individual. This is an important and valuable development. But the weakness of common-law rights is that they are not secure. Like any other rule of domestic law, they can be overridden by legislation. This is why advocates of international human rights law regard them as insufficient. They are afraid that populist pressures may lead to illiberal and oppressive measures. They are suspicious of the electoral majorities that ultimately control democratic legislatures. They therefore assert that some fundamental rights should have a higher status than ordinary laws, so that they cannot readily be dislodged politically, even with the authority of democratic legislatures.

In principle, democracies can enact whatever rights they want. The object of human rights law is to ensure that they get certain rights whether they want them or not. To achieve that, however, it is necessary to identify some other source of legitimacy for these rights, apart from the wishes of the population. There has to be some transcendent authority independent of the collective arrangements by which people govern themselves. In a more religious age than ours, this was perfectly straightforward. Rights were part of the moral law, ordained by God. In a totalitarian state, it is equally straightforward. Rights, so far as they exist at all, are ordained by the ruling group in accordance with its ideology. But in a secular democracy, what is it that makes rights legitimate, if not the decisions of representative bodies? What is the source, independent of popular endorsement, that enables us to identify some rights as so fundamental that they must not be removed or limited by political decision?

Rights do not exist in a vacuum. They are the creation of law, which is a product of social organisation, and therefore necessarily a matter of political choice. They are also claims against society, which for that reason call for a measure of social consent. So, when we speak of some rights as inherent in our humanity, we are not really saying anything about the nature of humanity. We are making a personal moral judgement that some rights ought to be adopted by human communities because they are so fundamental to their values and so widely accepted as to be above legitimate political debate. Almost all of us believe that there are some rights in that category. But the idea only works if the rights in question are truly fundamental and generally accepted. If there is room for reasonable people to disagree about them, then we need a political process to resolve that disagreement. In that case, they cannot be above legitimate political debate, except in a totalitarian state.

There are probably only two categories of right that are truly fundamental and generally accepted in that sense. First, there are rights which are fundamental because without them social existence is not possible. Without freedom from arbitrary detention, physical injury or death, without equality before the law and without recourse to impartial and independent courts, life would be nothing more than a crude contest in the deployment of force. Second, there are rights without which a community cannot function as a democracy. So there must at least be freedom of thought and expression, assembly and association, and the right to participate on equal terms with everyone else in fair and regular elections. Of course, democracies should confer many more rights than these. But they should confer them by collective political choice, not because they are thought to be inherent in our humanity or to derive from some transcendent law. And they should be open to repeal or restriction in the face of competing public interests which our representative institutions regard as more important.

Today, the main source of human rights in Britain is an international treaty, the European Convention on Human Rights. A great deal of our law is based on international treaties, more perhaps than most people realise. But treaties come in different shapes and sizes. Some of them deal with nuts-and-bolts problems that can only be effectively resolved internationally: for example, the safety of ships and aircraft or the insolvency of multinational companies. Some of them deal with human activities that are such a gross affront to our civilisation that every state should have a common approach to them: for example, torture or genocide. It is a basic principle of British constitutional law that international treaties have no effect on people's legal rights or duties without an Act of Parliament. In theory, this means that Parliament always has the last word on the contents of our law, even when it originates in a treaty. There is, however, one category of treaties that largely escapes Parliamentary control. I will call them dynamic treaties. A dynamic treaty is one that does not just say what our domestic law should be, but also provides a supranational mechanism for altering and developing it in future. The result is to transfer an essentially legislative power to an international body standing outside the constitutional framework of the United Kingdom, in other words outside the collective mechanisms by which we consent to the laws which govern us. By far the most significant dynamic treaties affecting Britain are the Human Rights Convention and the treaties constituting the European Union.

The European Union is a system of pooled sovereignty. Member states transfer decision-making power over important areas of their national life to the institutions of the European Union, including a European Commission, a European Court and a European Parliament in which each state is represented. They do this because in some areas collective action by a group of states is more effective than action taken by each of them separately. It is not very different from the principle on which the thirteen colonies of North America came together to form the United States in 1787. It involves a partial loss of national autonomy. It also removes decision-making to a more remote level at which national solidarities are weaker, bureaucratic direction less sensitive and democratic accountability at best indirect. This may or may not be a price worth paying for its advantages, but that is another issue. The Human Rights Convention is a very different thing. It is nothing to do with the European Union. It was drafted in the aftermath of the Second World War, under the shadow of the Gestapo and the concentration camps of the Third Reich. The draftsmen included prominent British lawyers, steeped in the common-law tradition, whose influence can be seen on every page. It has been adopted by the forty-seven states of the Council of Europe, many of which are not members of the European Union. The Human Rights Convention is not a regime of pooled sovereignty. It is an international code of law. For those who believe that fundamental rights should exist independently of democratic choice, human rights treaties have an obvious attraction. They create a source of law that does not depend on national decision-making processes.

The Human Rights Act 1998, which came into force in 2000, gives effect to the Human Rights Convention in British law. It empowers the domestic courts to strike down any rule of common law, regulation or government decision which is found to be incompatible with the Convention. It requires the courts to apply muscular principles of interpretation to statutes with a view to making them conform with the Convention. They do this even if the result is inconsistent with a natural reading of the language or with anything that the legislature can reasonably be supposed to have intended.

If muscular interpretation of this kind is not possible, then an Act of Parliament can be declared incompatible with the Convention, which is a signal to Parliament to repeal or amend it. Crucially, the Human Rights Act requires the British courts to take account of the rulings of the European Court of Human Rights, the international court set up in Strasbourg to interpret the Convention. The Strasbourg court generates law on a prodigious scale. In the six decades of its history, it has handed down some 21,600 decisions. The annual output of the court has increased exponentially in the past two decades. At the end of 2018, more than 56,000 cases were awaiting decision in Strasbourg. Very few of these cases were brought against Britain. In fact, Britain has one of the best records of any Convention country. It has featured in just over 2 per cent of cases where a violation of the Convention has been found. However, the British courts have to have regard to the entire body of Strasbourg case law, whether Britain was a party or not. In theory, the British courts could reject decisions of the Strasbourg court. In rare cases they do. Occasionally, Strasbourg modifies its position in response. But defiance is not really an option if Strasbourg persists. That would put Britain in breach of international law, something which on long-standing constitutional principle the domestic courts should avoid if they possibly can.

The Human Rights Act has been described as a 'constitutional' statute. It is not a supreme source of law prevailing over all others in the way that, say, the Constitution of the United States is. Parliament could repeal it by a majority of one in each House. But the description is a fair one in a slightly looser sense. Under the Act, the Convention prevails over every source of law other than Parliamentary statutes, and requires the courts to modify the operation even of Parliamentary statutes. While the Act remains in force, it ties the United Kingdom to a dynamic system of law whose development is the task of a court standing entirely outside its own political institutions. Unlike the legislation of the European Union, Britain has no political input into this process. The Convention and the case law of the Strasbourg court create a body of law which cannot be repealed or amended by Parliament short of withdrawing from the treaty altogether. The Act has been with us for less than twenty years. But in that short space of time it has had a transformative effect on our law. In some ways, its effect has been positive. The Act has protected the interests of vulnerable groups, with no natural body of support among the electorate or the press. It has forced more humane and inclusive values on ministers and officials. It has obliged decision-makers to listen to the objections of people whose interests are adversely affected, and to provide a coherent and objective justification for their decisions. All of these advantages are, however, capable of being provided by domestic law without recourse to an international treaty.

The British are traditionally averse to being told what to do by foreigners, an attitude often written off as insular nationalism. But the main reason for disquiet, at any rate among the more thoughtful critics of human rights law, is nothing to do with national prejudice. It is the impact that the European Convention and the Human Rights Court have had on the way that we make laws for our society. The Convention was originally conceived as a partial statement of rights universally regarded as fundamental: no torture, no arbitrary killing or imprisonment, freedom of thought and expression, due process of law and so on. It was not originally designed as a dynamic treaty. It was the Strasbourg court which transformed it into a dynamic treaty in the course of the first two decades of its existence. Its doctrine has been that the Convention is what it calls a 'living instrument'. The court develops it by a process of extrapolation or analogy, so as to reflect its own view of what additional rights a modern democracy ought to have. Now of course the court would not need to do this if the additional rights were already there in the treaty. It only needs to resort to the living instrument doctrine in order to declare rights which are not there. It is fair to say that some development of the text is unavoidable when applying an abstract statement of principle to concrete cases. In addition, some concepts in the Convention, such as the notion of 'inhuman or degrading' treatment, plainly do evolve over time with changes in our collective values. But the Strasbourg Court has gone much further than that.

Article 8 of the Convention is probably the most striking example of this kind of mission creep. Article 8 protects the human right to private and family life, the privacy of the home and of personal correspondence. It was designed as a protection against the surveillance state in totalitarian regimes. But the Strasbourg court has developed it into what it calls a 'principle of personal autonomy'. Acting on this principle, it has extended Article 8 so that it potentially covers anything that intrudes upon an individual person's autonomy. A very similar development has occurred in the United States courts in relation to the right to liberty under the Fourteenth Amendment. It will be obvious that most laws seek to some degree to intrude on personal autonomy. They impose standards of behaviour that people would not necessarily accept voluntarily. This may be illustrated by the vast range of issues which the Strasbourg court has held to be covered by Article 8. They include the legal status of illegitimate children, immigration and deportation, extradition, criminal sentencing, the recording of crime, abortion, artificial insemination, homosexuality and same-sex unions, child abduction, the policing of public demonstrations, employment and social security rights, legal aid, planning and environmental law, noise abatement, eviction for non-payment of rent and much else besides. All of these things have been included in the protection of private and family life. None of them is to be found in the language of the Convention. None of them is a natural implication from its terms. None of them has been agreed by the signatory states. They are all extensions of the text which rest on the sole authority of the judges of the Strasbourg court. This is, in reality, a form of non-consensual legislation.

The law that has emerged from this system is applied by the Strasbourg court in all forty-seven countries that have signed up to the Convention, with only very limited allowance for differences between their moral values, their political culture or their institutional traditions. Indeed, as a result of a series of controversial decisions of the court, parts of it are applied to military operations by Convention countries in non-Convention states such as Iraq and Afghanistan for which the Convention was never designed and to which it is ill adapted. Yet what is needed in order to protect human rights is not necessarily the same everywhere. Much depends on the strength of a country's political and administrative culture. The practical problems are not the same in a country recently released from half a century of autocratic government by a one-party state or a country in the throes of a violent religious war as they are in a country such as ours, with robust traditions and long experience of the rule of law.

I am not complacent about our human rights record. Britain has a strong libertarian tradition. Where we have departed from our own standards, there has usually been a good reason for doing so. But we have done some things which are morally and politically indefensible. In my lifetime, for example, Parliament has twice responded to political violence by authorising internment without trial in peacetime. So I have no problem about the idea of an international court to act as an external check. But most of the rights which the Strasbourg Court has added to our law are quite unsuitable for inclusion in any human rights instrument. They are contentious and far from fundamental. This has transformed the Convention from an expression of noble values, almost universally shared, into something meaner. It has become a template against which to assess most aspects of the ordinary domestic legal order, including some highly disputable ones. The result is to devalue the whole notion of universal human rights.

Many people will feel that some at least of the additional rights invented by the Strasbourg court ought to exist. I think so myself. But the real question is whether the decision to create them ought to be made by judges. Judges exist to apply the law. It is the business of citizens and their representatives to decide what the law ought to be. Many of the issues thrown up by the Convention are not even issues between the state and the citizen. They are really issues between different groups of citizens. This applies particularly to major social or moral issues such as abortion, foetal tissue research or medically assisted suicide, about which opinion is divided. In a democracy, the appropriate way of resolving such disagreements is through the political process. If I say that we should recognise a human right in appropriate cases not to be evicted from a council house for non-payment of rent, and you say that someone who has not performed his side of the bargain should have no such right, then the only alternative to a political resolution of our difference is to invite the judges to legislate. The main problem about modern human rights law is that it does this too readily. It transforms controversial political issues into questions of law for the courts. In this way, it takes critical decision-making powers out of the political process. Since that process is the only method by which the population at large is able to engage, however indirectly, in the shaping of law, this is hard to justify. If we are going to deal with fundamental human rights in a way that has such radical implications, then we need to have a very clear idea of what a fundamental human right really is. In particular, we have to distinguish a fundamental human right from something that is merely a good idea.

It is often pointed out that Parliament has authorised this way of making law by passing the Human Rights Act. And, of course, so it has. What is more, in 1998, when it did this, the expansive tendencies of the Strasbourg court were already apparent. But not everything that a democratic Parliament does is consistent with a democratic constitution. Parliament could abolish elections. It could ban opposition parties. It could forbid criticism of official policy. It could transfer its powers to a dictator, as the German Parliament did in 1933 and the French one in 1940. Decisions of this kind would have the authority of a democratic Parliament. But they would hardly be democratic. So, the fact that Parliament has incorporated the Convention into our law does not relieve us from the need to look at its implications for our democracy.

The problem can be most clearly seen in decisions about qualified Convention rights. Most Convention rights are qualified. They are subject to exceptions for cases where an interference with the right is judged to be 'necessary in a democratic society' for some legitimate purpose. According to the Convention, legitimate purposes include the prevention of crime, the protection of public health, the economic well-being of society and a number of other important public interests. If a national measure interferes with a protected right, the courts ask whether the interference has a legitimate purpose and, if so, whether that purpose is important enough to justify the interference. Ultimately, as the Appellate Committee of the House of Lords held in 2007, the Convention requires them to strike 'a fair balance between the rights of the individual and the interests of the community'.*

The Strasbourg court tends to give a wide scope to the rights protected by the Convention, as we have seen with Article 8. It does this precisely in order to require more and more legislative and governmental measures to be justified in court. The result is that in the courts most arguments about the Human Rights Convention are not about the existence of the rights in question but about the operation of these exceptions and qualifications. This poses in an acute form the problem of the role of judges in a democracy. Who is to decide what is necessary in a democratic

---

*Huang v. Secretary of State for the Home Department [2007] 2 AC 167, at para. 19.

society? Or what purposes are legitimate? Or what the prevention of crime, or public health, or the economic well-being of society require? Or what is a fair balance between the individual and the community? These are all intensely political questions. Yet the Convention reclassifies them as questions of law, thus removing them from the realm of democratic decision-making and referring them instead to national and international courts.

Domestic courts have occasionally expressed surprise and dismay at decisions emanating from Strasbourg. But their own legislative instincts are at least as strong. In the previous chapter I drew attention to the growing propensity of British judges to challenge the policies underlying legislative and governmental decisions. Human rights law has placed in their hands a powerful tool for doing that across a vastly expanded range of issues.

In 2014 the Supreme Court had to deal with one of the most sensitive and controversial moral issues of our time: assisted suicide for terminally ill patients. Our society is divided about this. What is life worth when one's ability to enjoy it has gone? Does human autonomy entitle an individual to assistance in killing himself? Always, or only sometimes? Are these just questions for the patient, or does society have an interest of its own? The Strasbourg court had previously held that the whole issue was culturally and politically too sensitive to permit of a single pan-European answer. Each Convention state would have to decide it in accordance with its own values. The essential issue for the Supreme Court was 'Who should give Britain's answer: Parliament or the courts?' Parliament had already given Britain's answer. The Suicide Act 1961 says that assisting someone to kill himself is a crime. Parliament has considered proposals to change the law on a number of occasions, but it has always decided against it. Yet five of the nine judges who sat on the appeal thought that the question was ultimately for the courts. Two of the five would have declared that the Suicide Act was incompatible with the Convention. The other three decided not to, but only because it would be premature until after Parliament had considered the matter. One of the three even threatened that unless Parliament 'satisfactorily addressed' the issue, the courts might do it for them. If this threat meant anything, it meant that the courts should be prepared to exercise legislative powers in place of the legislature if it is dissatisfied with the legislature's response.* I am not alone in questioning the constitutional propriety of all this. The meaning of the Suicide Act is a question of law. But whether the Suicide Act is a good thing is not a question of law. It is a question of

---

*R *(Nicklinson) v. Ministry of Justice* [2015] AC 657.

legislative policy and ultimately of moral and political opinion. I was one of those who considered that this was entirely a matter for Parliament. I thought that on such an issue as this, my own opinion had no greater weight by virtue of my judicial office than that of any other citizen. I still think so.

There is a large body of judicial and academic opinion which would justify the majority's view on the ground that judges simply make better law than legislatures. Maybe they do, although the historical record is rather patchy. But it is not enough for law to be 'good' or 'better'. In a democracy, the public must in some sense 'own' it. Law must have the legitimacy which only some process of consent can confer. The difficulty is that there are usually no conclusive criteria for deciding what constitutes 'good' law. I may regard as very bad a principle which you consider to be wholly admirable. Our difference may not be capable of being tested on wholly objective criteria. It may be due to the fact that we have different moral or political starting-points. Let me give a specific illustration, taken from a recent decision of the Supreme Court. In 2018 the Court had to consider the statutory ban on abortion in Northern Ireland. I have no desire to defend the ban, which was long ago repealed in the rest of the United Kingdom. But I am not presently concerned with its merits, only with the question by what process its merits should be decided in Northern Ireland. The issue on the appeal turned on the compatibility of the law with Article 8 of the Human Rights Convention. In particular it turned on the exception in Article 8 for measures 'necessary in a democratic society [...] for the protection of health or morals'. The President of the Court (speaking for herself, for the court was divided) thought that no weight at all should be given to the 'democratic judgement of the Northern Ireland Assembly', which had decided against changing the law. She justified this view by observing that the courts were as well qualified to decide such matters as the legislature. 'In fact, in some ways, the courts may be thought better qualified, because they are able to weigh the evidence, the legal materials, and the arguments in a dispassionate manner, without the external pressures to which legislators may be subject.'* This is a particularly interesting statement of a view which is widely held by lawyers but rarely expressed so candidly. The problem about it is that it treats the formation of a society's legislative policy as a purely technical question, a matter of evidence and forensic argument. In fact, abortion is not a technical question. It is a profound moral issue between different bodies of

---

Re Northern Ireland Human Rights Commission's Application for Judicial Review [2019] 1 All ER 173, at [38].

opinion in Northern Ireland. They take opposing views about the relative importance of a woman's personal autonomy and the preservation of the life of an unborn child. There is no doubt about what the law is. The question is what it ought to be. This is an inherently legislative question, calling for a political resolution. Yet there is no room in the President's approach for collective moral values, or indeed for any moral values other than those of the judges. Democratic choice and Parliamentary sentiment are relegated to the status of mere 'external pressures', as if there was something wrong with legislation being influenced by public opinion.

Judicial attitudes are not monolithic and not immovable. Over the last ten years, the Strasbourg court has undoubtedly become somewhat more sensitive to the political implications of its decisions and less aggressive in its expansion of Convention rights. British judges too have shown signs of retreating from some of the advanced positions that they occupied a few years ago, on assisted suicide among other things. My own view is that a fundamental change of judicial approach would be far preferable to the only realistic alternative, which is to withdraw from the Convention and replace it by a purely domestic legal instrument that left the last word to Parliament. It remains to be seen whether either of these things will happen. In the meantime, in both the Strasbourg court and the domestic courts the propriety of legislative and governmental decisions on issues falling within the broad scope of the Convention will continue to be treated as a question of law, and therefore ultimately for the courts to decide. Certainly, the views of Parliament will sometimes be a factor, but no more than that and no more than sometimes. How much attention the courts should pay to them will be a matter of judicial value-judgement.

The implicit message is that even in a democracy such issues are not, in the last analysis, for the representatives of the general body of citizens. From time to time, the Strasbourg court has said this out loud. It has twice held that the statutory rule in Britain that serving prisoners cannot vote is incompatible with the Convention. The interesting thing about these decisions is the way that the court dealt with the fact that the rule had been enacted by Parliament. In its first decision, in 2005, Strasbourg said that Parliament cannot have thought properly about the human rights implications.* In the second, in 2012, it could not say that, because the House of Commons had by then debated the 2005 decision and reaffirmed its original view. So Strasbourg simply said that it

---

* *Hirst v. United Kingdom (No 2)* (2005) 42 EHRR 849.

was a question of law, and not for Parliament at all.*
There is an obvious irony in the Strasbourg court's
rejection of Parliamentary authority in the name of
democratic legitimacy.

Yet that irony brings us close to the heart of
the matter. We are in the presence of two rival
conceptions of democracy. One is that democracy
is a constitutional mechanism for arriving at collective decisions and accommodating dissent. The
other is that it is a system of values. After the end
of the Second World War, the democratic label was
claimed by the autocratic communist states more
or less forcibly established by the Soviet Union in
eastern Europe, such as the German Democratic
Republic. What they meant by democracy was a value-based system, in which communism was treated
as inherently democratic, although not chosen or
necessarily supported by the people or even open
to meaningful debate among them. The values of
the Strasbourg court are, of course, very different
from those of the post-war dictatorships of eastern
Europe. But they have this much in common. They
both employ the concept of democracy as a gener-
alised term of approval for a set of political values.
The choices of elected representatives are only
legitimate within the limits allowed by those values.

---

* *Scoppola v. Italy (No 3)* (2012) 56 EHRR 663.

Democracy is a word with a strong emotional resonance. Everyone wants to appropriate it as a label for their preferred positions. It is particularly difficult for people to acknowledge that a true democracy may sometimes espouse truly illiberal policies. So we distort the language, not in order to deceive but to avoid confronting awkward dilemmas.

This is not just a question of vocabulary. Democracy in its traditional sense is a fragile construct. It is vulnerable to the idea that one's own values are so obviously urgent and right that the means by which one gets them adopted do not matter. That is one reason why it exists in only about half the world's states. Even in those states, it is of relatively recent origin and its basic premises are under challenge by the advocates of various value-based systems. One of these is a system of law-based decision-making that would entrench a broad range of liberal principles as the constitutional basis of the state. Democratic choice would be impotent to remove or limit them without the authority of courts of law. It is a model in which many lawyers ardently believe. So much so that they find it genuinely difficult to understand that there can be legitimate objection to it, even from liberal thinkers. The objection is that the claim of liberal values to privileged constitutional status is conceptually no different from the rather similar claims of communism, fascism, monarchism, Catholicism, Islamism and all the other great -isms that have historically claimed a monopoly of legitimate political discourse, on the ground that their advocates considered them to be obviously right. Yet, other models are possible. One can believe in rights without wanting to remove them from the democratic arena by placing them under the exclusive jurisdiction of a priestly caste of judges. One can believe that one's fellow citizens ought to choose liberal values without wanting to impose them.

IV

LESSONS FROM AMERICA

When the French political scientist Alexis de Tocqueville visited the United States in the 1830s, one of the things that struck him most forcibly was the dominant place occupied by lawyers in the public life of the nation. In his classic account of early American democracy, De Tocqueville suggested that lawyers as a class had succeeded to the beliefs and the influence of the old landed aristocracy. They shared its habits and tastes and, above all, its contempt for popular opinion.

> The more we reflect upon all that occurs in the United States, the more we shall find that the lawyers, as a body, form the most powerful, if not the only counterpoise to the democratic element of the constitution. [...] There is scarcely any political question in the United States that does not ultimately resolve itself into a judicial question.

There was only one other country that De Tocqueville could think of where the legal elite enjoyed a comparable influence over public affairs, and that

country was Britain. A new edition of De Tocqueville, rewritten for today, would probably make the
same point.

Why do we believe in democracy, or think
we do? What are the proper limits of democratic
choice? What rights should a democratic constitution protect, even against the will of the people?
When the British argue about these questions, they
generally look to the United States – sometimes as
an inspiration, sometimes as a warning. Yet in spite
of a close similarity of political outlook, the American constitutional tradition is the polar opposite of
the British one. At its most basic level, the difference
is between two models of the state: a legal model
and a political one. The Constitution of the United
States is the archetypal legal constitution. Britain
by comparison has historically been the archetypal
political state. In both countries, as well as in much
of Europe, we have witnessed a mounting tide of
hostility to representative politics over the past three
decades. This has naturally been accompanied by
a growing interest in the legal model. The United
States is not, of course, its only exemplar. Almost
every constitution in the world has adopted the legal
model, and most of them have been strongly influenced by the American prototype. Constitutions are
not just formal documents. They come with habits
and attitudes which form over many years to make

them workable. It is even more difficult to replicate these habits and attitudes than to make a new constitution. But at a time when many British judges are inching their way towards their own concept of fundamental law, the experience of the United States is worth examining. For the legal model raises dilemmas in a democracy of which the United States has a longer and more varied experience than any other country.

The prime purpose of any constitution is to provide a framework of political rules for making collective decisions. In its original form of 1787, the Constitution of the United States did almost nothing else. The protection of rights came later, with the ten amendments of 1791 which together constitute the Bill of Rights. Twelve years later, in 1803, came the decision in *Marbury v. Madison*, which established the power of the Supreme Court to quash Acts of Congress held to be unconstitutional.* So, by the beginning of the nineteenth century, the US Constitution had already acquired the three basic features which have come to be regarded as the hallmarks of every legal constitution. First, there is a written code of rights, which prevails over all other law. Second, it is proof against political amendment, except by some extraordinary procedure. In the United States

---

*5 US 137 (1803).

three-quarters of the states must ratify it. Other countries require a super-majority in the legislature or a popular referendum. Third, it confers on judges the power to enforce constitutional rights, striking down any act of the state, including its legislation, which they find to be inconsistent with them. The very broad terms of some clauses of the US Constitution leave a great deal of latitude to the judiciary in performing this function.

In the taxonomy of national constitutions, the polar opposite of the American Constitution was probably the Constitution of the French Fifth Republic as it was originally conceived by General de Gaulle and his adviser René Cassin in 1958. France is the historic home of public law. The Conseil d'État, which stands at the apex of a system of administrative tribunals, dates back to Napoleon. But French administrative tribunals had traditionally been concerned with standards of administration and not with governmental or legislative policy. One of the great objects of the Gaullist constitution was to avoid the 'rule of judges', which the general regarded as one of the more deplorable features of American public life. He was particularly opposed to the idea of a French Supreme Court with power to test legislative or governmental action by reference to fundamental principles. 'The only Supreme Court in France', he observed, 'is the people.' Since

1958 the gap between the United States and Europe has narrowed. Specialised constitutional courts now exist in all major countries of the European continent including France. Law has become a much more significant restraint on state action. The constitutional courts of Germany, Italy and France are said to have struck down or revised more laws in the last half-century than the US Supreme Court has done in its entire history.

By comparison, in Britain, at any rate as a matter of orthodox constitutional doctrine, there are no constitutional limits on the power of Parliament. There is no fundamental law that Parliament cannot alter or abrogate at will. Even the legislation of the European Union, which has prevailed over domestic legislation since 1973, did so only by virtue of an Act of Parliament which could be repealed at will, as we have seen. Our unwritten constitution treats the powers of the state as matters for decision by Parliament as the occasion arises. The exercise of those powers is the function of ministers answerable to Parliament and ultimately to the electorate. We are almost the only country in the world of which this is true.

Of course, the difference between the legal and the political models of the state has never been absolute. Almost all constitutions have elements of both. The United States has developed a sophisticated doctrine of the separation of powers, which reserves a large space to political judgements by the executive and the legislature. In Britain, law has always had a place in its basically political constitution. Nonetheless, the conceptual difference between the legal and the political model remains a real one, which exposes two very different views about democracy.

The attraction of the legal model is that it is based on a body of principle, applied by judges whose perceptions are less likely to be swayed by passion, prejudice, self-interest or *Realpolitik* than those of politicians or voters. But its patronising overtones are plain. The legal model seeks to create a body of constitutional rights that is beyond the reach of democratic choice. Its advocates do not trust elective institutions to form opinions about them with the necessary restraint, intelligence or moral sensibility. They therefore favour an accretion of power to the sort of people, namely judges, whose superior qualities and independence of public opinion are thought to produce more enlightened decisions. 'We the people' are the opening words of the US Constitution. But, as James Madison's contributions to the *Federalist Papers* show, the founding fathers regarded the people as a bigger threat to liberty than their governments. Madison looked for a solution in the representative principle. He expected lawmakers to be wiser and more circumspect than their electors.

For later generations, however, the representative principle has not been enough. As electorates expanded with the democratisation of the west, the pressure of popular prejudice became stronger. So there were calls for constitutional limits on what democratic legislatures could authorise. Distrust of elected majorities and fear of majoritarian tyranny has always been the driving force behind the idea of entrenched constitutional rights.

It is true that the decisions of voters and their representatives are not morally pure. They are based on a variable mixture of wisdom and folly, of prejudice and understanding, of idealism, pragmatism and self-interest. The real question is whether this is a good enough reason to constrain their choices by law. To answer that question, I think that we have to ask ourselves why we believe in counting votes at all. There are, surely, two main reasons. In the first place, all governmental authority that is not based simply on force requires some source of legitimacy. If a political community is to have any long-term stability, people must have a reason to obey laws that they do not like, other than the threat of coercion. 'We the people' is the emotional foundation of democracy in Britain as well as the United States, even if the British do not have a document that says so. The second reason why we believe in counting votes is that it reflects our sense of social and political equality.

Thomas Jefferson wrote in one of his letters to the German scientist Alexander von Humboldt that 'lex majoris [the law of the majority] is the fundamental law of every society of individuals *of equal rights.*' The critical words of that formulation were the last ones: 'of equal rights'. The interests and opinions of citizens conflict. We cannot all have our own way. But we can expect the decision-making process to treat our various interests and opinions with equal consideration and respect. That is achieved by giving all of us an equal share in decision-making even if, as individual voters, our personal influence on the outcome is minimal. A constitution that was based not on democratic choice but on some embedded scheme of values, such as liberalism, human rights, Islamic political theology or the dictatorship of the proletariat, would not achieve this. It would privilege those citizens who happened to agree with these values. That might not matter if the values in question were universally, or almost universally, accepted. But you do not need to entrench values in the constitution if they are universally accepted. You only need to entrench them if they are controversial and therefore liable to be discarded by people with a free choice in the matter.

This suggests that the essence of democracy is not moral rectitude but participation. The proper function of a constitution is to determine how we participate in the decision-making process, and not to determine what the outcome ought to be. Whether voters act from good or bad motives is not the point. We cannot make a constitution for some imaginary world in which people are without prejudices or indifferent to their own interests. All that a political system can really aspire to do is to provide a method of decision-making that has the best chance of accommodating disagreements between citizens as they actually are. This calls for a political process in which every citizen can engage, whose results, however imperfect, are likely to be acceptable to the widest possible range of interests and opinions. This is arguably a more important priority for a political community than finding the right answer to its moral dilemmas – even assuming that there is a right answer or that we can finally hit on it. The problem about the legal model is that it marginalises the political process. When a judge identifies something as a constitutional or human or fundamental right, he is saying that it derives from a higher law than the ordinary decision-making processes of the state. He is declaring that its existence and extent are not to be determined by political choice.

Yet many judicial decisions about fundamental rights are themselves political choices, only made by a smaller and unrepresentative body of people. In an American context, the most interesting example is probably the Due Process clause of the Fourteenth Amendment. The Fourteenth Amendment was one of a number of amendments passed in the 1860s in the aftermath of the Civil War. They were mainly directed against slavery. The Due Process clause provides (among other things) that no state shall deprive any person of liberty without due process of law. Successive decisions of the US Supreme Court have made this the functional equivalent of Article 8 of the European Human Rights Convention, which protects private life. Both provisions have been interpreted as potentially embracing any interference with the personal autonomy of individuals, within limits. But within what limits? All mandatory rules of law interfere with the personal autonomy of individuals. That is what they are for. If the limits to the right to liberty are to be fixed as a matter of principle by judges, the answer must necessarily depend on a judgement about which interferences with personal autonomy are acceptable and which are not. By what standards is such a judgement to be made?

Half a century ago, this question was energetically debated in the US Supreme Court in a celebrated case about a Connecticut statute forbidding contraception. The Court was unanimous in its view that this was a particularly foolish law. We may all agree with that. But foolish laws are not unconstitutional for that reason alone. The Court held by a majority that there was a constitutional right of privacy, which the Connecticut statute violated. This right is, however, nowhere mentioned in the Constitution, and confusion about its exact basis is evident from the diversity of opinion among the justices. Some thought that a right of privacy existed because it was analogous to other rights specifically mentioned in the Constitution. Some thought that the right was to be derived from the collective values of the people as the Court perceived them to be. One thought that it was enough to say that a right of privacy was implicit in the whole concept of liberty. The dissenters said that there was no such right, because the only basis on which it could be said to exist was that enough justices thought that it was a good idea.* I think that the dissenters had a point. When a judge is asked to decide a question as broad as this, the issue is not really whether the right exists but whether it ought to exist. Yet that is surely a question for lawmakers, not judges.

Over the century and a half since it was added to the Constitution, the Due Process clause has been the basis of some of the most illiberal as well as the most progressive decisions of the federal courts, according to the outlook of the judges

---

Griswold v. Connecticut 381 US 479 (1965).

of the day. As is well known, during the so-called Lochner era between the 1890s and the 1930s, US federal courts struck down as unconstitutional some 150 pieces of employee protection legislation under the Due Process clause. They did this on the ground that liberty required absolute freedom of contract, subject only to considerations of public policy. Among the laws that they struck down were state laws limiting hours of work in the interests of health, guaranteeing a right to join unions and outlawing child labour. Moving to the opposite political extreme, the Due Process clause was also the basis of the decision in *Roe v. Wade* in 1973. The US Supreme Court derived a right to an abortion from the newly discovered constitutional rights of privacy and autonomy.* The same reasoning lay behind the Court's decision on same-sex marriage in 2015.† In both cases, the Court's decisions were necessarily based on the perception of the justices that this was what liberty now required. Yet it seems likely that if the same issues had come for the first time before the court as it is now constituted, the result would have been different, although nothing would have changed other than the outlook of individual justices. One is bound to question whether decisions so

---

*410 US 113 (1973).

†*Obergefell v. Hodges* 135 S. Ct. 2584 (2015).

sensitive to the personalities and preferences of nine individuals can really be described as law.

Two lessons can be drawn from the broad range of outcomes which at different times have been justified under the Due Process clause. One is that on politically controversial issues, the decisions of judges almost always involve a large element of political value judgement. The case for or against labour regulation is a question of economic and social policy. The case for or against abortion is a question of social and moral values. What liberty requires in either context, and how far it should go, are fundamentally political questions. The other lesson is that judicial decisions on issues like these are not necessarily wiser or morally superior to the judgements of the legislature even if they are made by a more transparent procedure. In Britain, the courts are today regarded as bastions of liberalism against governments in thrall to illiberal public opinion. But before the Second World War they were regarded as allies of predatory capitalism, deeply hostile to organised labour and public social provision. All advances in these fields were achieved politically, by legislation. Much of the employee protection legislation struck down by the federal courts in the Lochner era had been on the statute book in Britain since the middle of the nineteenth century. It had got there by political action.

The justification commonly put forward for

treating such matters as constitutional issues and referring them to judges is that it protects minorities against majoritarian tyranny better than the legislative process. I question whether there is any factual basis for this assumption. The most that can be said is that in some periods of history it has done so, and in others it has not. What constitutes majoritarian tyranny very much depends on how you define your minority and what you regard as tyranny. Except perhaps in classic discrimination cases, where the animating principle is to treat like cases alike, there are no legal standards by which these questions can be answered. The only available standards are political. Experience suggests that judges charged with making essentially political decisions are no more likely than politicians to make enlightened ones.

There is also, perhaps, a wider issue, namely, whether it is wise to make law in this way. It is true that partisan divisions and institutional blockages in Congress have made controversial legislative change difficult to achieve in the United States. This inevitably encourages those who look for a judicial resolution of major social issues. But the chief function of any political system is to accommodate differences of interest and opinion among citizens. Resolving these differences by judicial decision contributes nothing to that end. On the contrary, characterising something as a constitutional right removes the issue from the arena of political debate and transfers it to judges. In the United States it does this irreversibly, unless the Supreme Court changes its mind or the constitution is amended. The debate about abortion conveniently illustrates many of these themes. I am in favour of a regulated right of abortion. But I question whether it can properly be treated as a fundamental right, displacing legislative or political intervention. Abortion was once just as controversial in Britain as it still is in the United States. After extensive Parliamentary debate, it was introduced in 1967 by ordinary legislation, within carefully defined limits and subject to a framework of clinical regulation. The same pattern was followed in Europe, where all but one state (and Northern Ireland) have now legislated for a regulated right of abortion. As a result, abortion is relatively uncontroversial in Europe. I suspect, although I cannot prove it, that one reason why abortion remains so controversial in the United States is that it was introduced judicially: i.e., by a method that relegated the wider political debate among Americans to irrelevance. This has distorted American politics by turning Presidential elections into a contest for the power to appoint politically dependable justices to the Supreme Court. The results were apparent in the undignified and partisan positions taken at Justice Kavanagh's confirmation hearings in 2018.

In his first inaugural address, in 1861, Abraham Lincoln drew attention to the implications of filling the gaps in the constitution by judicial decision. His words are well known:

> The candid citizen must confess that if the policy of the government upon vital questions affecting the whole people is to be irrevocably fixed by decisions of the Supreme Court, [...] the people will have ceased to be their own rulers, having to that extent practically resigned their government into the hands of that eminent tribunal.

Lincoln had in mind the notorious decision of the Supreme Court in the Dred Scott case, which had held that African Americans were not to be treated as citizens.* But he was also making a broader point, which was about active citizenship. A nation cannot hope to accommodate divisions among its people unless its citizens participate in the process of finding political solutions to common problems. Law has its own competing claim to legitimacy, but it is no substitute for politics.

I am not saying that there are no rights which should be constitutionally protected in a democracy. But I think that one lesson which Britain can learn

---

Dred Scott v. Sandford 60 US 393 (1857).

from US experience is that one must be careful about which rights one regards as so fundamental as to be beyond democratic choice. I have argued that there are only two kinds of rights that are truly fundamental in that sense. They are rights to a basic measure of security for life, liberty and property, and rights such as freedom of expression, assembly and association, without which a community cannot function as a democracy. These rights will not be enough to prevent majoritarian tyranny. But no code of rights can do that. The law simply has no solution to the problem of majoritarian tyranny, even in a system of perfectly entrenched constitutional rights like that of the United States. Law can insist that public authorities have some legal basis for everything that they do. It can supply the basic level of security on which civilised life depends. It can protect minorities identified by some personal characteristic, such as gender, race or sexual orientation, from discrimination. But the courts cannot parry the broader threat that legislative majorities may act oppressively, unless they assume general legislative powers for themselves. The only effective constraints on the abuse of democratic power are political. They depend on active citizenship, on a culture of political sensitivity and on the capacity of representative institutions to perform their traditional role of accommodating division and mediating dissent. If that no longer happens in the United

States, or to some extent in Britain, it is because a large section of the population no longer wants it to. On critical issues, our political culture has lost the capacity to identify common premises, common bonds and common priorities that stand above our differences. Politics may be a dirty word, but the alternative to it is bleak: a dysfunctional community, lacking the cohesion to meet any of its social or economic challenges and exposed to mounting internal and external violence. This is a potential catastrophe in the making. But there is nothing that law can do about it.

In an essay written in 1942, the great American judge Learned Hand confessed that he could not predict whether the spirit of equity and fairness which animated the constitution would survive without judges to enforce them. But he added these words, which encapsulate the dilemmas of the legal constitution:

> this much I think I do know – that a society so riven that the spirit of moderation is gone, no court can save; that a society where that spirit flourishes, no court need save; that in a society which evades its responsibility by thrusting upon the courts the nurture of that spirit, that spirit in the end will perish.*

---

* 'The Contribution of an Independent Judiciary to Civilisation' (1942), reprinted in the *Spirit of Liberty* (1953), pp. 118ff., at p. 164.

V

CONSTITUTIONS,
NEW AND OLD

'For 150 years, power has been deposited in Parliament, and for the last sixty or seventy years [Parliament] has been becoming more and more unpopular.' The thought sounds familiar. But the author was not a leader writer in a daily paper or a demonstrator in Parliament Square. It was Benjamin Disraeli, perhaps the only true genius ever to rise to the top of British politics. He put them into the mouth of his hero Sidonia in his novel *Coningsby*. *Coningsby* was published in 1844, at a time of great constitutional ferment in Britain, and on the eve of a political crisis in some ways very like the present crisis about Brexit. Of course, Sidonia was Disraeli himself, and his diagnosis was bleak. The peril of England, he said, lay not in laws and institutions but in what he called 'the decline of its character as a community'. Without a powerful sense of community, even the best laws and institutions were a dead letter. I cite these lugubrious words in order to make a number of points. First, there is nothing new about our current political predicaments. Second, in any political crisis there will always be calls for changes to our institutions. Third, the suggested changes are usually irrelevant to the problem that has provoked them. Even so, Disraeli's warning has never discouraged people from calling for institutional reform, when the real problem is in ourselves. For quite a few years now, these calls have taken the form of proposals for a written constitution.

I have been concerned in this book with our persistent habit of looking for legal solutions to what are really political problems. Calls for a written constitution mark the extreme point of this tendency. Theoretically, we could have a written constitution without expanding the constitutional role of judges. As I have pointed out, the Constitution of the French Fifth Republic, in its original form of 1958, came pretty close to that. But in practice every scheme of constitutional reform suggested for Britain in recent years has sought to limit the powers of Parliament and government, and to increase those of judges. This is not an accident. A written constitution is by definition a supreme source of law. It prevails over ordinary Parliamentary legislation. Any supreme law that sets out to regulate relations between the citizen and the state must necessarily put some rights of citizens beyond the reach of the elected legislature. But the power that the legislature loses under such schemes does not just disappear. It passes to judges. Judges recognise, interpret and sometimes create constitutional rights. Judges decide when these rights may be trumped by other public interests. It will be apparent from earlier chapters that I am sceptical about claims that our system of government can be improved by injecting a larger legal element into it. The main problem about such claims is that they attribute our current political malaise to the defects of our institutions when they are actually due to other causes which no amount of institutional reform will cure.

As it stands, the British constitution has four features that distinguish it from nearly every other constitution in the world. First, it is unwritten. There is no fundamental document against which the constitutionality of acts of the government or the legislature can be measured. Second, there is only one truly fundamental constitutional rule, which is that Parliament is sovereign. There is no legal limit to what it can do. The only limits are political. Since the House of Commons, as the dominant element in Parliament, is an assembly of elected representatives, the sovereignty of Parliament is the foundation of our democracy. Third, the limits on what Parliament can do depend on political conventions. Conventions are not law but rules of practice. They derive their force from shared political sentiment, which would make it politically costly to disregard them. Some of them are fundamental: for example, the convention that the monarch must act on the advice of her ministers,

that the monarch may not veto Parliamentary legislation, that the House of Lords does not obstruct
legislation for which the government has an electoral mandate or that Parliament will not normally
exercise its undoubted right to legislate for Scotland
or Wales on matters that have been devolved to their
local legislatures. It has been said that, while the US
constitution is a matter of law, the British constitution is a matter of opinion. This is too glib, but there
is some truth in it. Fourth and last, the government
is part of Parliament, and dominates it without ever
being entirely in control of it. Its dominant position
is due partly to tight party discipline and partly to
the size of the ministerial vote. But the main reason
is the long political tradition, reflected in its proce-
dural rules, that Parliament is not just a legislative or
deliberative body but an instrument of government.
It is there to support the executive or to change it
for another which it can support. The first three of
these features were reaffirmed in the Supreme Court
decision of 2017, which ruled that the government
needed Parliamentary authority to give notice to
withdraw from the European Union.* The fourth,
the executive's control of the Parliamentary agenda,
has been severely tested by the parliamentary crisis

R (Miller) v. Secretary of State for Exiting the European Union
[2018] AC 61.

over Brexit, because a minority government which had failed to obtain Parliamentary sanction for its proposals attempted to use it to stifle discussion of any alternative. But in more normal circumstances it seems likely to remain a critical feature of our Parliamentary system.

The objections to these arrangements are that they are obscure, old-fashioned, out of step with international practice and give far too much power to Parliament. There is some justice in all of these criticisms. But before we look for alternative arrangements, we need to understand how we ended up with the present ones. The unlimited sovereignty of Parliament is a legal idea, but the law did not create it. Politics created it. Historically, sovereignty resided in the Crown. The monarchs gradually, and on the whole peacefully, ceded their personal power to Parliament and to ministers who governed in their name but were answerable to Parliament. The law never assumed a political role. It merely acknowledged the political facts. Nothing has ever happened in Britain to create a new source of law to stand above Parliament. The British constitution is unique, but uniqueness is not necessarily a vice. It is the result of our history, which is itself unique. Across the world, the godparents of written constitutions have been revolution, invasion, civil war and decolonisation. Constitutions have almost always been adopted upon the foundation of the state or the destruction of some previous order. As a result, there was always a blank sheet of paper on which to write them. But Britain is an ancient state with a long and unbroken constitutional history. It cannot be reduced to a blank sheet of paper. For more than three centuries, it has been fortunate, or perhaps unfortunate, in having experienced none of the catastrophes that have called for new beginnings elsewhere.

You do not have to believe, like Charles Dickens's Mr Podsnap, that our constitution was bestowed on us by a benign providence, to be wary of projects to demolish and rebuild it. Nations are prisoners of their past. They can discard it, but only at the cost of immense disruption and unpredictable outcomes. Britain has developed institutions that go with the grain of its long experience. A written constitution could no doubt be devised which would be an artefact of perfect rationality, a thing of great intellectual beauty. But it would have no basis in our historic experience, and experience counts for a great deal in human affairs: more than rationality, more even than beauty. Ultimately, the habits, traditions and attitudes of human communities are more powerful than law. Indeed, they are the foundation of law.

If our existing informal constitution was intolerable, we might have to put up with the disruption and instability involved in jettisoning it. But in fact, it has brought us real advantages. Because it remains essentially a political and not a legal constitution, it is capable of significant incremental development without any formal process of amendment. This has meant that the British state has sometimes experienced significant constitutional change without really intending it. But it has also enabled the state to adapt to major changes in our national life which would have overwhelmed more formal arrangements: the political marginalisation of the monarchy, the onset of industrialisation and mass democracy, the existential crises of two world wars, the creation and then loss of a worldwide empire, the rise of powerful nationalisms in Ireland, Scotland and Wales. All of this has been accommodated politically, without changing the basic constitutional framework.

Devolution is probably the outstanding recent example. It has radically altered the internal workings of the United Kingdom. But it was achieved politically, by ordinary legislation after a general election in which it was part of the successful party's manifesto. Compare Britain's accommodation of Scottish and Welsh nationalism with Spain's apparent inability to accommodate the nationalism of the Catalans. One reason why the issue has been so much more confrontational in Spain is that relations between the state and its constituent regions are fixed by Article 2 of the Spanish constitution. The Spanish constitution is independently enforceable by the judges and, like all formal constitutions, it is hard to amend. A political solution is therefore difficult to achieve. The fact that Britain has recently been through a period of radical change and is entering another is not therefore a reason for ditching our current constitutional arrangements. On the contrary, it is a reason for retaining them. Crises of political legitimacy are not unusual, either here or elsewhere. Other democracies have handled them no better and often worse than we have, in spite of having elaborate formal constitutions with all the features recommended by those who would like to see one here.

This suggests, as Disraeli argued in *Coningsby*, that we should be looking at more fundamental causes of the current diseases of our body politic than the peculiarities of our constitution. I have argued that a stable democracy requires a minimum level of public engagement with the political process. This is where the real problem lies. The British are not apathetic about politics. Successive annual surveys published by the Hansard Society and *British Social Attitudes* show us to be a country with a strong sense of civic obligation and a real interest in public affairs. Yet this has been accompanied by a progressive disengagement from the actual political process. The symptoms are all around us: the long-term decline in the membership rolls of all major national political parties; falling turn-out at elections; widespread contempt for professional politicians; the rise of powerful regional nationalisms offering a more immediate source of legitimacy. These things are not quirks of our political system. Other countries with very different systems have experienced them too. Membership of political parties has declined across most of Europe. The decline has been steepest in countries such as the UK, France and Sweden, with the longest democratic traditions. Regional nationalisms have challenged established states in Belgium, Spain and elsewhere. Turn-out rates at presidential elections in the United States hit a post-war peak in the 1950s and 1960s, but have fallen ever since. They are currently among the lowest in the world. France has recently experienced an even sharper fall-off.

These are symptoms of a wholesale rejection not just of politicians but of the political process itself. Why has this happened in a country as politically aware as ours? Of course, there have been spectacular incidents such as the scandal that erupted in Britain in 2009 over Parliamentary expenses. Those who have always believed in a formal constitution have tended to seize on such moments as indicating a general institutional breakdown that might justify a new start. But such suggestions have never got very far. This is because there are more fundamental factors at work which are nothing to do with the peculiarities of our constitution. They are inherent in the democratic process itself.

Democracy generates unrealistically high expectations. These expectations spring partly from the eternal optimism of humankind, partly from a misunderstanding of the role of politicians and partly from an exaggerated view of their power to effect major change. All of these problems are aggravated by the auction of promises at every general election. When these expectations are disappointed, as they inevitably are, a sense of impotent frustration undermines public confidence in the whole political process. Either the prospectus was false or the execution was incompetent.

This does not necessarily matter when everything else is going well. But it matters extremely when they are going badly. Functioning democracies have always been heavily dependent on economic good fortune. Western democracy has had plenty of it. It was born in the nineteenth century, in an age of creative optimism, economic expansion and European supremacy. Except for two short periods, the United States has enjoyed continuously rising levels of prosperity, both absolutely and relative to other countries, until quite recently. In the life of any community, the shattering of optimism is a dangerous

moment. Disillusionment with the promise of progress was a major factor in the thirty-year crisis of
Europe which began in 1914 and ended in 1945. That
crisis was characterised by a resort to autocracy
in much of Europe with appalling consequences
for the wellbeing of the continent and its peoples.
Three-quarters of a century have passed since 1945,
years marked by rapid economic growth and expo-
nential improvements in standards of living. But
today, most western democracies face problems of
faltering growth and relative economic decline, of
redundant skills and capricious patterns of inequal-
ity, most of them the legacy of past successes.
These things generate feelings of disempowerment
which have tended to discredit democratic institutions. The polling data collected by the authoritative
World Values Survey suggest that, although most
of Europe still regards democracy as fundamental,
in Britain, France and the United States only the
older generation agree. Most people under thirty no
longer do. Recent polls conducted by the Hansard
Society show that a clear majority of our fellow
citizens would welcome government by a strongman willing to break the rules. A high proportion
think that this strongman should not be inhibited
by representative institutions such as Parliament.
Some climate change activists have openly proposed
a suspension of democracy on the ground that

their programme for limiting carbon emissions and species extinction will never be endorsed by electorates. Ironically, this is happening at the very moment when in most advanced economies voters are finally beginning to grasp the scale of the challenge and the urgency of addressing it, even at the expense of current consumption.

Public resentment of democratic institutions has been aggravated by the perceived remoteness of politicians. Representative democracy necessarily produces a political class, separated by outlook and usually by lifestyle from those who vote for them. This is inherent in the practical exigencies of public life. Few politicians will ever be like the generality of their electors, even if they began that way. The financial rewards of a political career are not very great. But getting elected calls for exceptional levels of ambition and commitment. The practice of legislation and government calls for a great deal of information, experience and skill. These qualities are unlikely to be shared by most of the electorate. The truth is that all political systems are aristocracies of knowledge. Democracy is only different in that the aristocracies are installed and removable by popular vote. This radically affects the way that they behave and think, generally for the better. But it does not bring them any closer to their electors.

All of this is hard to reconcile with current

notions of representation, which have undergone a subtle but important change in our lifetimes. People expect their representatives not just to act for them, but to be like them. This is an old idea. John Adams, one of the Founding Fathers of the United States, thought that the legislature should be 'an exact portrait in miniature' of the population. The French revolutionary leader Mirabeau declared that it should represent the people as exactly as a map represents a landscape. But these arresting images represent the top-down rhetoric of a political elite. The idea has acquired a much wider resonance in our own age, which rejects deference and abhors hierarchy in a way that neither Adams nor Mirabeau would have understood. Resentment of political, administrative and academic elites played a large part in the British referendum campaign of 2016. 'Britons have had enough of experts', a prominent politician famously declared while it was in progress. And not only Britons. Similar resentments were decisive in the American presidential campaign later that year, as well as in the French presidential campaign of 2017 and the Italian legislative elections of 2018. In all of these contests, lack of political experience was a central part of the successful candidates' electoral pitch. It remains to be seen whether this will produce higher standards of government or greater responsiveness to public concerns. Expertise is fallible, but it does not follow that it is worthless or that ignorance is better.

Britain's recent experience is not unique. But the consequences of rejecting political insiders are more serious in Britain than in other countries. This is because of the critical role of political parties in Parliament and the intimate relationship between the government and the House of Commons. Party membership may have dwindled to low levels, but party members still choose Parliamentary candidates and have a major voice in the choice of party leaders. Declining membership rolls have allowed both of the big national parties to be colonised by relatively small numbers of hard-edged zealots and entryists with a very limited vision of the public interest and no interest at all in accommodating anyone else. This process reached its ultimate extreme in Britain in the summer of 2019, when the Prime Minister of a major western democracy with an electorate of about 47 million, was to be chosen by an atypical and self-appointed group of about 150,000 members of a political party with no absolute majority in the House of Commons and dwindling support in the country at large.

Even among the wider public, people are less willing to accept the horse-trading that is a neces-sary part of building any kind of public consensus. This absolutist approach to controversial issues is the hallmark of fanatics. But it is not confined to them. Few things were more revealing than the electoral catastrophe that befell the Liberal Democrats in 2015. They lost out because of the compromises that they had had to make to create a viable coalition government in 2010, when no party had a majority in the House of Commons. To many of their erstwhile supporters, compromise was inherently unprincipled. Unbending attachment to one's principles can be morally attractive. But it is often politically sterile.

This is not just our problem. The United States has for the moment ceased to be a political community because neither side of the major political divide respects the legitimacy of policy positions with which it disagrees. In Britain, we have reached the same position on Brexit. In the last French presidential election the successful candidate, Emmanuel Macron, was preferred by less than a quarter of the electorate in the first round. A shift of just 3 per cent of the votes would have resulted in a run-off between the intransigent right of Marine Le Pen and the intransigent left of Jean-Luc Mélenchon. Two and a half millennia ago, Aristotle regarded democracy as an inherently unstable form of government, precisely because it was vulnerable to demagogues like these. The genius of modern western representative democracy has been to defy that prediction for some two centuries. But for how much longer?

If this is a plausible assessment of our current problems of political legitimacy, then it must be obvious that adopting a written constitution to serve as our supreme law will not make much difference. It will bring about two main changes, neither of which is self-evidently desirable. First, it will replace our highly adaptable constitution by something that is more rigid and less capable of accommodating the unexpected. And, second, it will produce a partial shift of power from an elective and removable aristocracy of knowledge, to a corps of judges that is just as remote, less representative and neither elective nor removable. None of this means that there should be no constitutional change. There has been a great deal, and there will be more. But it has been gradual and piecemeal. It has not involved the replacement of our constitution by a new code. And it has not undermined the sovereignty of the elected Parliament which is the basis of our democracy.

The one significant change that might be thought pressing harks back to the points which I have made about public engagement with politics. It concerns the electoral system. The 'first past the post' system that applies to Parliamentary elections in the United Kingdom has advantages that are often overlooked. It enables governments to come to power with absolute majorities in the House of Commons even when they have no absolute majority among the electorate at large. Indeed they may not even have the largest number of votes. This is a much criticised feature of our system. But it has contributed greatly to the stability of the English state and to the ability of governments to take decisive action when it was needed. It has, however, achieved this by squeezing out minor parties, unless they have a strong regional base. The result has been to confer an alternating monopoly on the two biggest national parties. This was probably acceptable at a time when the two major national parties had large membership rolls and a high proportion of British voters identified themselves with one or other of them. But it is difficult to justify now. Their membership base is smaller and less representative than it has ever been. A move to proportional representation at Parliamentary elections would weaken the duopoly. It would encourage more and smaller parties. It would give the established national parties a stronger incentive to broaden their appeal beyond their base. It would force them to negotiate coalitions when they could not get enough electoral support to enable them to govern alone. A system of open primaries for choosing Parliamentary candidates would break the power of the tiny activist minorities who control local party associations. These changes would mean that the process of policy adjustment and compromise, which currently operates mainly within political parties, would operate between political parties. That would probably mean weaker and less stable governments, which would be a real loss. But it might be a price worth paying if it boosted public engagement and enabled politics once more to accommodate differences of interest and opinion across our population.

There is already plenty of gloomy speculation about how long democracy can last against an adverse economic background, without my adding to it. Prophets are usually wrong. But one thing I will prophesy. We will not recognise the end of democracy if it comes. Advanced democracies are not overthrown. There are no tanks on the streets, no sudden catastrophes, no brash dictators or braying mobs. Instead, their institutions are imperceptibly drained of everything that once made them democratic. The labels will still be there, but will no longer describe the contents. The façade will still stand, but there will be nothing behind it. The rhetoric of democracy will be unchanged, but it will be meaningless. And the fault will be ours.